The Brief History of World War 2 in Asia

The Asia-Pacific War, the Eastern Fleat, Pearl Harbor and the Atom Bomb that Shocked Japan (1941-1945)

Disclaimer

Introduction

World **War II** in **Asia** (also called **Pacific War**, (and) *Pacific War*) was fought in East Asia and the Pacific Ocean between the Japanese Empire and a coalition of Allies, the most important of which were the United States, China, and (from August 1945) the Soviet Union.

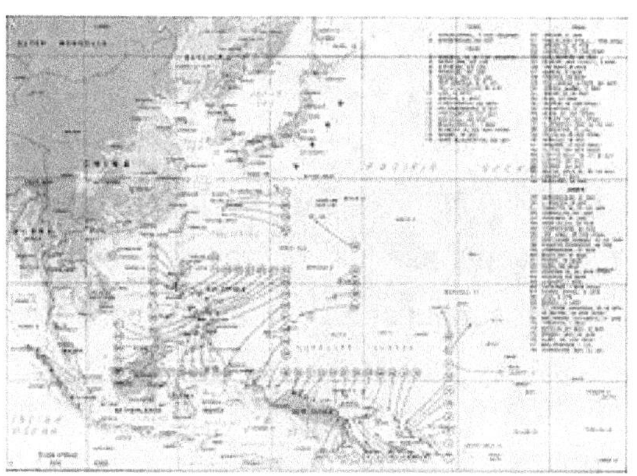

Even years before World War II began in Asia, there were signs of growing unrest:

- The United States and the European powers (Britain, France, and the Netherlands) colonized many islands and countries in Asia, gaining dominion over much of the Asian population.

- Japan began to grow in strength: because of its more westernized economic plans, Japanese industry, as well as its military, developed rapidly.
- There was growing unrest in China, so Japan could easily gain a lot of influence there.

Japan, since its opening to the world in the 19th century, had become a highly industrialized country, ruled by the military and an emperor considered a deity.

However, the country faced a major problem: it had a large population surplus and few raw materials for its industry. Therefore, the Japanese had increasingly turned to imperialism, the conquest of new territory for Japan in Asia.

Yet over the years the attitude of the Japanese changed: at first they only wanted small expansions to save their territory from overpopulation, but later they wanted much more: their own empire in Asia. They wanted to remove the oppressors (the colonial powers) from Asia and establish their own authority in its place, and they also wanted control over China.

The first steps were taken in the 19th century when the Japanese army occupied the islands south of the mainland, including Okinawa. In the First Sino-Japanese War (1894-1895), Formosa (Taiwan) and Korea were taken from China and annexed to Japan, and in the Russo-Japanese War (1904-1905), the Russians lost their naval base at Port Arthur to the Japanese, who thus effectively gained control of the Yellow Sea. In World War I, the Japanese captured much of the German colonial empire in Asia, including the Mariana Islands, Marshall Islands, and the Gilberts Islands. At the Treaty of Versailles, Japan got all the conquered islands north of the equator.

In the period after the First World War, the US, the Netherlands, France, Great Britain, Australia and New Zealand jointly tried to counter Japan's growing influence and expansion. Japan, which in the 1930s came under the growing influence of ultra-nationalist, expansionist militaries, increasingly aligned itself with the Axis powers.

Table of contents

Sino-Japanese War

Manchuria had been an independent state separate from China since the First Sino-Japanese War, serving as a buffer state between Japan and China. On September 18, 1931, north of the city of Shenyang, a railway line owned by part of the Japanese government was blown up. Japan blamed Chinese nationalists, invaded Manchuria and established a Japanese vassal state, Manchukwo, there in 1932. The ex-Chinese emperor Xuantong (Pu Yi) was appointed head of state, although he had little power; the Japanese basically ruled.

Japan then invaded China itself in 1937. Japanese troops occupied Jehol province south of Manchuria. China would not budge and cede even more territory to Japan, and Japan only wanted to conquer more Chinese territory. Jehol was annexed to Manchukwo as an administrative unit, and soon Shanghai and Beijing also fell into Japanese hands. The Japanese conquered a large part of eastern China. The capture of the Chinese capital Nanking was followed by the Nanking Massacre, in which hundreds of thousands of inhabitants were murdered.

This invasion caused the US, together with the Dutch East Indies, to institute an oil boycott against Japan, which they considered an aggressor. This put Japan in a difficult economic situation: without the oil supplies that came annually from the U.S. and the Dutch East Indies, Japan would only have oil for eighteen months, and when that was over Japan would be completely paralyzed. The Americans also imposed trade boycotts on scrap iron, steel, and jet fuel. These restrictions cut Japan off from the raw materials it needed. The Japanese Emperor Hirohito therefore wanted to drive the Allies out of the Pacific Ocean through a mighty offensive and set up a great Japanese-Asian empire.

In 1938 a border conflict broke out for Manchukwo between Japan and the Soviet Union, with the main battles being the Battle of Lake Chasan (1938) and the Battle of Halhin Gol, both of which were won by the Soviet Union. This conflict ended with a non-aggression pact in 1941 and Japan's reluctance to keep its eye on Siberia and the Urals any longer, allowing Joseph Stalin to mobilize all his Siberian armies against the subsequent German invasion.

Japanese sphere of influence before the war

At the outbreak of World War II in 1939, Japan already controlled a large area, much larger than present-day Japan. The actual Japan then included:

- Japan itself
- the Koerilen
- the southern half of Sakhalin Island
- Okinawa
- Iwo Jima
- Taiwan (Formosa)
- Korea.

In addition, there were the mandate areas it had acquired after World War I (the South Pacific Mandate Area):

- the Marshall Islands.
- the Mariana Islands (minus Guam, which was American)
- the Gilberts Islands
- Micronesia
- the Palau Islands

There were also the occupied territories in China, such as Manchuwko and Nanking, where a Chinese vassal state was founded called Japanese-China.

In Southeast Asia, after the fall of France in Europe, French Indo-China (the present states of Vietnam, Laos and Cambodia) was ceded to Japan, which at the same time had Thailand on its side under occupation.The Japanese wanted to establish a great Asian empire. This would include the following areas that were not yet in Japanese hands:

- Dutch East Indies
- The British colonies in Borneo
- Malacca
- Burma
- British India (present-day India, Bangladesh and Pakistan)
- China
- Mongolia
- All Soviet territory east of Lake Baku.
- American possessions in the Pacific: Philippines, Wake, Guam, Midway and Hawaii
- Australia

- New Zealand
- The Free French Possessions

Attack on Pearl Harbor

On September 27, 1940, Japan signed the Three-Power Pact with the Axis powers Germany and Italy. The countries promised each other military support in case one of them would be attacked.

To eliminate the powerful navy of their main opponent, the Americans, the main goal of the Japanese was to attack the American naval base Pearl Harbor in Hawaii. Here the entire American fleet was anchored in the Pacific Ocean, close together and therefore an ideal target.

Japan sent its seven aircraft carriers along with two fleet squadrons to Pearl Harbor, via the Northwest.

Without an official declaration of war, the surprise attack followed on 7 December 1941. More than 200 American planes were destroyed, many cruisers sunk or seriously damaged and over 2400 Americans killed, compared to the loss of 29 planes and 5 submarines on the Japanese side. However, most American ships were not sunk but only severely damaged, and many sailed again several months later and even participated in the Battle of Midway.

In response to the attack the Americans carried out a direct bombing raid on Tokyo, the *Doolittle raid*. This attack did not cause much damage but was a bright spot that could boost the morale of the Allies after the many losses.

The Harbour

Located over 3,600 miles from San Francisco, Pearl Harbor was popular with American sailors. If the enemy sunk a ship in the harbor entrance, the base was unusable. To reach the open sea the fleet needed three hours. Once the fleet was in, along with all supplies and stores, it formed an attractive target. However, to fully mobilize the fleet and have it set sail would cost millions of dollars, and no commander wanted to risk giving such an order in vain.

Admiral James Richardson, commander of the base in May 1940, thought the ships belonged in safe harbors on the west coast. When he went to President Franklin D. Roosevelt with his objections, he was relieved of his post and replaced by Admiral Husband Kimmel.

Timeline until December 7, 1941

As early as October 16, 1941, the American media were aware of the imminent situation. They paid some attention to this threat in their news articles. However, the American people felt completely protected by their army and paid little attention to the articles. Henry Stimson, who at that time was Secretary of Defense in America, was well aware of the threat, because in response to the news articles he said: *Now is a time to wait, so that Japan can make the first move, after which we can attack them directly*.

Japan and America were still negotiating with each other, but these were not going well. On November 5, six messages were intercepted stating that the negotiations with America should be completed by November 25.

The leader of the Japanese war operation, Yamamoto, wanted to control the whole South Pacific area and therefore he developed a strategy to attack Pearl Harbor, the Philippines and all other non-Japanese places in this area at the same time. He presented his plan on November 7 and called it Plan Z.

Plan "Z"

Nobody in the Japanese Navy knew Pearl Harbor better than Yamamoto. In his cabin on his flagship Nagato hung a map of the base on which he had made all kinds of notes. Because everything on the base was done with a fixed regularity, he could know when he would find the largest concentration of ships there. The anti-aircraft defences were insufficient and he believed that an air attack had a good chance of success. He was inspired by admiral Heihachiro Togo and named his plan after his Z-signal during the battle of Tsushima (1905).

He knew that twenty-four British planes sunk three battleships on 11 November 1940 during an attack on the Italian fleet at Taranto, with a loss of only three aircraft. The Americans also recognized the importance of this attack, but Admiral Kimmel refused to install anti-torpedo nets because they would hinder the freedom of movement of his ships.

Japanese tactics

Yamamoto preferred to put the battleships out of action first because he thought this would be a hard blow to the Americans. When he presented his plan to attack Pearl Harbor with planes that would take off from aircraft carriers to captain Minoru Genda, a specialist in air attacks, he was advised to attack the American carriers because they were the biggest threat to the Japanese Imperial Navy.

Japan had two of the world's largest aircraft carriers: the *Akagi* (36,500 tons) which could carry 91 aircraft (larger than the American *Lexington* and *Saratoga*) and the 38,200-ton *Kaga*. Together with the *Hiryu*, *Soryu*, *Zuikaku* and *Shokaku* the Japanese Imperial Navy had six aircraft carriers. Genda planned to use all six in the attack (441 aircraft in total) along with an advance force of submarines. Torpedoes were preferred because they were more powerful and accurate than bombs.

Although Yamamoto wanted to command the attack himself, he could not do so because he had too many other responsibilities. The choice fell on Rear Admiral Chuichi Nagumo. He was not an expert on aircraft, but was appointed because of his seniority. He was dismayed to hear of the responsibility of his task, but consoled himself with the thought that the attack might not go ahead. After all, Japan was not yet at war with the US. Moreover, the plan had yet to be approved by Japan's Supreme Command.

Doubts about Plan Z

Emperor Hirohito was kept in the dark by his ministers and generals about their concrete plans to eliminate the American base at Pearl Harbor. On 5 September 1941 the emperor granted Prince Konoe an audience, in which he was horrified to learn that preparations for war took precedence over diplomacy. Thereupon he immediately summoned some high-ranking officers, General Sugiyama and Admiral Nagano, to clarify matters. They assured him that they still preferred a diplomatic solution. The next day, at the Imperial Conference, the matter came up again. When asked whether preparations for war were preferable

to diplomacy, Sugiyama and Nagano kept quiet and let others do the talking.

Then something happened that almost never happened. The emperor, who was supposed to preside over the conference and not actively participate in the deliberations, rose from his chair and took the floor:

We very much regret that the Supreme Command did not see fit to clarify the matter for us.

He quoted part of a poem:

Since we are all brothers in this world, why are the waves and winds so restless?

After this very gross breach of protocol, there was a minute-long silence during which the company tried to come to terms with their Emperor's unexpected outburst. Finally Admiral Nagano took the floor and assured Hirohito of their loyalty to the emperor, that they understood the importance of diplomacy and that they regretted having displeased the emperor with their behaviour. The meeting then closed in what Konoe said was a very tense atmosphere.

Yamamoto had presented his plan to Genda and later to the Navy, but had met with much resistance from the latter. Many felt that the plan was too bold. Yamamoto was convinced that if it came to war, America would have to be dealt a devastating blow so that Japan could occupy the Philippines, Malacca, and the Dutch East Indies unopposed before the American Navy could recover. His colleagues still assumed the decisive power of battleships of which Japan had two in the pipeline: the Yamato and the Musashi.

Timeline to December 7, 1941 (continued)

Despite the decision to execute plan Z, Japan still negotiated with America to try not to arouse suspicion. On 10 November a negotiation proposal was sent to Cordell Hull, at that moment the American Secretary of State. The Americans, however, ignored this proposal and so ten days later a new proposal was made by Saber Kurusu, the Japanese negotiator. Also, the deadline that had been scheduled for November 25 was moved to November 29.

Because of the looming situation, the American Secretary of Defense again made a striking statement: *The question is how we should maneuver them into the position of firing the first shot, without too much danger and damage to ourselves.* (The question is, how we should maneuver them into the position of firing the first shot, without too much danger and damage to ourselves). This again shows that America was well aware of the threat and also wanted war, without being 'guilty'.

The Japanese media wrote that on November 25, the old end date, a large fleet had left the Japanese port. According to them, it was sailing partly towards the Philippines and partly towards the Strait of Formosa, southeastern China. In reality, the fleet left only a day later. On that day, Nagumo, the vice admiral of the Japanese fleet, left Hitokappu Bay (単冠湾, *Hitokappuwan*) on the east side of Etorofu with 6 aircraft carriers, 423 aircraft, 2 battleships, 28 submarines, 2 cruisers and 11 destroyers. It is clear that the aircraft carriers were relatively heavily over-represented in this fleet, but that was logical, because the intention was to attack with the aircraft carriers. The other ships had only the task of protecting these precious warships. From the outset there was a strict radio silence between the ships, so that the Americans would not easily notice and trace them.

In response to Kurusu's proposal on 20 November, Hull presented a counterproposal. However, his demands were so high that it was already clear that Japan would not comply. Another indication that America was trying to start a war without making the first move. One day after Hull's proposal, America's Secretary of War Henry Stimson sent messages to the Pacific fleet. In them he warned of possible hostile action by Japan.

Japan felt that after the failure of diplomatic avenues there was no alternative but war. Nevertheless, they still conducted negotiations with America to make it appear that there was still an intention to pursue the diplomatic path.

Some people within the American government wished new warnings of a threat of war to be sent out, but the military leadership refused, fearing false alarms. Yet from then on there were more and more silent indications of an attack. For example, the FBI intercepted a message about an impending war, but ignored it, because they did not want to create panic among the population.

Because of the increasingly clear threats of war, the U.S. Navy decided that it would not allow itself to be attacked without being ready. Therefore, they sent an aircraft carrier toward Midway, northwest of Hawaii. Two other aircraft carriers were sent to another area. All these ship moves showed again that America was aware of the threat from Japan. Despite these measures, they were not yet alert enough, as would be seen later. By then it was already December 5.

On December 6, an American telegrapher deciphered some Japanese messages that had been intercepted several days earlier. The deciphering made it clear to him that there were again indications of war, but his chief wanted nothing to know about it. On the contrary, he demanded that the telegrapher put this message to rest. Instead of getting ready for an imminent war, the idea of supporting England if it was attacked by Germany was now being considered.

On December 6, Hirohito, then Emperor of Japan, received a message from the Japanese-Pacific fleet. This message was quickly answered. On December 7, at 10:32 a.m. and 12 seconds local time, Franklin D. Roosevelt read that

Japan had **not** declared war on America, but had come to the conclusion that further negotiations with America were pointless.

December 7

An hour after this message, the President read an (intercepted) message which stated that an official declaration of war was to be delivered to America at 1:00 p.m. It did not, however, give details of the place and time of an attack by Japanese forces. However, it did not give details of the place and time of an attack by Japanese forces. In response, Marshall ordered the Pacific fleet to be on extra alert.

By this same time, they noticed a mysterious Japanese submarine attempting to enter Pearl Harbor.

Some people were of the opinion that this submarine was 'lost', but a more logical explanation seems to be that it was looking for the weak spots within the American fleet and even more so to find out whether it was prepared for war at all. Anyway, around noon, this submarine was shot at by a destroyer and sunk.The officers at Pearl Harbor were not really afraid of this strange submarine. They reported the incident to headquarters very late.

At 12.02 hours the first wave of attacks by Japanese aircraft was detected by an American radar station. These were the planes that had taken off from the Japanese carriers at 11.00 hours. At 12:20 another radar again noticed this wave of planes, now closer to the harbor.

However, the duty officer ignored this frightening sight and warned no one, probably because a number of B-17s from the U.S. were scheduled to arrive that day.It was not until 12:25 p.m. that Kimmel was notified of the earlier incident with the submarine, but still no action was taken. All ships were anchored in the harbor, making them an extremely vulnerable target for the approaching aircraft.

At 12.49 pm the Japanese pilots received official permission for the attack; at 12.55 pm the first Japanese attack wave actually attacked Pearl Harbor from the northwest. The second wave followed more than an hour later, at 2 pm. They attacked the harbour from the northeast.

At 2:45 p.m., of the 96 ships in the harbor, 18 had been sunk or severely damaged. Also 188 of the 394 aircraft had been destroyed and 159 others damaged. A total of 2402 soldiers died as a result of this attack.

There were 1178 wounded. The high number of deaths was mainly caused by the sinking of the battleship USS *Arizona*. During the sinking of this ship 1177 people were killed.

Declaration of War by Nazi Germany

The fact that Japan and America were now at war was reason for Hitler to declare war on the Americans on the fourth day after the attack. The United States thus once again became involved in a European war (the first time was World War I), which it would have preferred to avoid.

Varia

The Japanese Navy, like Admiral Harold Rainsford Stark, the only American to warn of its possibility, would have been inspired for the attack by the British surprise attack by a squadron of Fairey Swordfish aircraft from the aircraft carrier *HMS Illustrious* on the Italian fleet at the Battle of Tarente on 11/12 November 1940. Stark warned of the possibility of such an attack in a memo on 22 November 1940, which would, however, be ignored by the rest of the US admiralty.

Conquest of Hong Kong

Already on the same day as the attack on Pearl Harbor, Hong Kong was attacked on the Chinese coast. Hong Kong was a British crown colony and an excellent naval port for attacks on the Japanese positions around Formosa and in China. The Japanese occupation of Canton and Hainan had previously encircled Hong Kong. In late November 1941, 3,000 Canadians joined the British garrison of Hong Kong which at that time numbered about 12,000 men.

The same hour as the attack on Pearl Harbor began, Japanese dive bombers also attacked Hong Kong with a devastating surprise bombardment. After this there was only fresh drinking water for one day, and Hong Kong had become an easy prey for the Japanese army. The Japanese infantry overran the citadel in the Kowloon district, the mainland district. On 18 December the British had to surrender this district to the Japanese. After only a few hours the Japanese had crossed the channel and landed on Hong Kong island. The bridgehead was quickly expanded and at the same time the British lines were infiltrated by a fifth column. On Christmas Day the garrison surrendered to the Japanese after stiff resistance.

Conquest of the Philippines, Malacca, Singapore and Burma

The Philippines, an American territory, was attacked by the Japanese in December 1941. The archipelago was forced to surrender by a series of amphibious attacks. Manila was declared an open city, and unopposed Japanese army units entered the Philippine capital. 80,000 American troops managed to retreat to stronghold Bataan and held their ground. American commander Douglas MacArthur was evacuated to Darwin, Australia, on March 11, 1942. Shortly thereafter, on May 8, the new commander General Jonathan Wainwright surrendered to the Japanese: 130,000 Allied troops were made prisoners of war and the Philippines became part of the Japanese empire.

The Battle of the Philippines

The **Battle of the Philippines** involved the invasion of the Philippines by Japan in 1941 - 1942 and the defense of the islands by Filipino and American forces. Although it resulted in a Japanese victory, the victors were delayed by the resolve of the defenders in other areas, as well as contributed to Allied counterattacks in the Southwest Pacific, beginning in late 1942.

It is considered the greatest military defeat the United States has ever suffered.

The defence

Beginning in mid-1941, after growing tension between Japan and some other powers, including the United

States, Britain, and the Netherlands, many countries in Southeast Asia began preparations for a possible war.

In December 1941, the combined defense forces in the Philippines belonged to the Philippine Army, commanded by General Douglas MacArthur, who had retired as U.S. Chief of Staff in 1937, and accepted command of the Philippine Army. MacArthur's task, given by the government of the Philippines, was primarily to reform and establish an army composed primarily of reservists. The army was severely lacking in equipment, training, and organization, among other things.

The US garrison, which consisted of 22,532 troops, also known as the Philippine Division, was commanded by Major General George Grunert. It consisted mainly of the U.S. Philippine Division, made up in part of a fairly large number of Filipinos, who served as scouts.

The garrison was reinforced by 8,500 Continental United States National Reserve troops, made up in part of the only armored units, two tank battalions.

The *US Army Air Corps Far East Air Force* (FEAF), commanded by Major General Lewis H. Brereton, was the largest US air formation outside the United States, consisting of 107 P-40 fighters and 35 B-17 bombers.

MacArthur organized the defenders into four different units. The *North Luzon Force*, commanded by Major General Jonathan M. Wainwright, defended the most logical points of attack for amphibious assault and the central plains. This area also included the Bataan Peninsula, the appropriate place to fall back to if necessary, which was located near Manila Bay.

Waintwright's forces consisted of the 11th, 21st, and 31st infantry divisions of the Philippine Army, the 26th U.S. Cavalry Division (a reconnaissance unit), a battalion of the 45th Infantry Division (also a reconnaissance unit), two batteries consisting of 144 mm guns, and a mountain gun. The Philippine 71st Infantry Division also served as a reserve and could only be deployed on MacArthur's orders.

The *South Luzon Force*, under Brigadier General George M. Parker Jr. was to control the zone east and south of Manila. Parker's force consisted of the 41st and 51st infantry divisions of the Philippine Army and two batteries of the U.S. 86th Artillery Division of (originally also a reconnaissance unit).

The 'Visayan-Mindanao *unit, commanded by Brigadier General William F. Sharp, consisted of the 61st and 81st infantry divisions of the Philippine Army and the 101st infantry division.*

A reserve unit, under MacArthur's direct command, was composed of the Philippine Division, the *Far East Air Force*, and units of Philippine Army and Philippine Division Headquarters, stationed north of Manila. Four American artillery regiments guarded the entrance to Manila, including Corregidor Island.

The dispute of the *Far East Air Force*

After the outbreak of war on 7 December 1941, Brereton encouraged his bosses to carry out bombing raids against Formosa, then Japanese territory and where it was quite possible that a Japanese attack would be launched, but his request was turned down.

This proved to be a big mistake, as there was too little anti-aircraft artillery in the Philippines, and FEAF was almost defeated on the ground, through aerial bombardment over the next few days.

The invasion

The Japanese 14th Army, commanded by General Masahary Homma, began its invasion by landing on the island of Batan (not to be confused with the peninsula of Bataan), north of Luzon, on December 8, 1941. That same day half of the American air force on Luzon was destroyed by Japanese air attacks, partly due to miscommunications on the American side and partly because the Japanese managed to surprise the Americans.

Landings on the mainland followed two days later, on December 10. With the destruction of the American air force, the Japanese had hegemony in the airspace from the beginning.

From December 11 to 23, most of Luzon fell into Japanese hands, followed by landings on the southern tip of Luzon, at Legazpi, as well as in the Gulf of Lingayen and on Mindanao.

Most of the Allied forces surrendered after a time, or were overrun by Japanese superiority. The Philippine Division of the US positioned itself in the landscape to cover the withdrawals of the troops, on their way to Bataan. This was also done from the standpoint of countering Japanese advances in the Subic Bay area. On 23 December

MacArthur informed his commanders in the field that he was reactivating a pre-war plan. This meant that he intended to defend only Bataan and Corregidor, both military headquarters and the Philippine government were moving towards Corregidor. Still a large number of forces remained in other areas for some months.

The battle of Bataan

On 30 December, the Philippine 31st Infantry Division moved toward the vicinity of Zigzag Pass to provide cover for the flanks of retreating forces from central and southern Luzon. The U.S. Philippine Division organized its positions at Bataan. The 31st Division then advanced to a defensive position on the western side of the Olongapo-Manilla road, near the intersection of Layac, in the north of the Bataan Peninsula, on 5 January 1942.

One was forced to surrender the crossroads on 6 January, but the retreat to Bataan was quite successful. The 31st Division took up a reserve position on the peninsula to recover from the losses of the firefights in the flanks.

From 7 to 14 January, the Japanese concentrated on reconnaissance and preparations for an attack on the overall defensive line of Abucay. Philippine and American forces managed to withstand night attacks near Abucay, on 10 to 12 January, and on 16 January units of the U.S. Philippine Division counterattacked. This proved unsuccessful, however, and the division was forced to retreat to a reserve position in the Cas Pilar-Bagec area on 26 January.

The Japanese, aware of heavy losses, undertook patrols and limited local attacks in the following weeks. As the Allied position kept having to be withdrawn, U.S. President Franklin Delano Roosevelt ordered MacArthur to move from Corregidor to Australia, as Supreme Commander of the Southwest Pacific. (MacArthur's famous speech on the Philippines, in which he said, "I came from the Bataan and I will return," was delivered at Terowie, South Australia on March 20).

Wainwright was given command of Allied forces in the Philippines on March 12. During this period, units of the U.S. Philippine Division were shuttled back and forth to defend other sectors as well.

Allied forces, now weakened by poor nutrition, disease and far too long exposure to combat, faced a new wave of attack from the Japanese from March 28.

On 3 April, the Japanese broke through the gaps in the Allied lines along Mount Samat. The U.S. Philippine Division, no longer operating as a coordinated unit, was unable to mount a counterattack against the enemy's fierce attacks. On April 8, the U.S. 57th Infantry Division and the Philippine 31st Division were overrun at the Alangan River. The US 45th Infantry Division finally surrendered on 10 April 1942.

Corregidor was now defended by 11,000 troops consisting of the U.S. 4th Marine Regiment, other infantry, U.S. artillery units, and U.S. Navy men deployed as infantry.

The Japanese began their attack on Corregidor with an artillery bombardment on May 1. During the night of May 5-6, two battalions of the Japanese 61st Infantry Regiment landed northeast of the island.

Despite a strong defence, the Japanese managed to form a beachhead which was soon reinforced by tanks and artillery. The defenders were quickly pushed back to the defensive position on Malinta Hill.

In the late afternoon of May 6, Wainwright asked Homma for the terms of surrender. Homma insisted that surrender must mean the surrender of all Allied forces in the Philippines. Since Wainwright believed that all the lives of those on Corregidor would be endangered, he agreed to the terms. On May 8, he sent a message to Sharp. He ordered him to surrender the Visayan Mindanao Unit. Sharp agreed but many individuals continued the struggle in the form of guerrilla warfare.

The surrender was the beginning of three and a half years of oppression of the Allied survivors. This oppression included the Bataan Death March and the extremely harsh living conditions of the Japanese concentration camps.

Allied forces began the campaign to retake the Philippines in 1944. This began with landings on the island of Leyte.

Importance

The defense of the Philippines was the longest-lasting resistance to the Imperial Japanese Army in the early stages of World War II. After the attack at Abucay, the Japanese limited themselves to siege operations while waiting for reinforcements and did not resume their attack until April, giving MacArthur forty days to prepare Australia as an operational base. The initial resistance in the Philippines gave Australia crucial time to organize for its defense. Filipino-American resistance to the Japanese until the fall of Bataan on 9 April 1942 lasted over three months.

In the British colonies of Malacca and Singapore the British defence was largely based on an attack by sea. On 8 December 1941 the Japanese landed on the east coast of the peninsula of Malacca (British colony, now part of Malaysia) The Japanese landed as close as possible to the important airfield Kota Bharu. A Japanese armoured division quickly moved westwards, hoping to cut off the British 11th Division. The latter however managed to retreat in time, leaving Penang harbour unprotected.

Preparation

The port city of Singapore was the main British naval port in the Pacific.The deep sea ports provided excellent access for heavy warships.The extensive port facilities provided facilities for repairs otherwise only available in the United States and Britain.

The island was heavily defended against a landing from the sea. It was considered the "Gibraltar of the East".

These facilities and its defences were known to Japan and the Japanese planners were plotting a landing in Malacca, for all the defences had been built against a landing from the sea, not against an attack through malarial-infested Malacca.

The peninsula itself was also of great value: it produced 43% of the world's tin. Malacca was also a major source of rubber. The rubber plantations were of great value to both sides; Malacca produced over 30% of the world's rubber. The rubber plantations were seen as so important that the British army was not allowed to practice here, or was allowed to practice only minimally.

In the years leading up to the Second World War the British devised various defence strategies. One of these was a response in case Japan attacked via Malacca: operation Matador. The plan also provided for an increase in the resources, especially over 670 aircraft, needed to repel a major Japanese attack. The British government reduced that number to 350. In Malacca a series of airfields were built for these planes. Churchill, however, gave priority first to fighting in the Battle of Britain, and later to assisting the Soviet Union and fighting in the Middle East.

Operation Matador also provided for a defensive incursion into southern Thailand to prevent a Japanese landing there. This task was entrusted to the 11th Indian Division of the Third Indian Army Corps, already responsible for the defence of northern Malacca. How this division was to perform two tasks simultaneously remained unclear in the plan.

The British commander did coordinate his defence plans with the Dutch defenders in the Dutch East Indies.

The Military Aviation of the Royal Dutch East Indies Army (ML-KNIL) had approximately 450 aircraft at its disposal, divided into several aircraft groups. The Dutch government had ordered a total of 144 Brewsters of types 339C and 339D. At the outbreak of war only 71 had been delivered, of which only about 50 were ready for use.

On 25 December 1941 all 9 Brewster 339D's of 2-VLG-V, together with all 12 pilots of the division, were sent to Kallang to help the British defend Singapore against the

Japanese. These fighters were equipped with bomb racks and could also be used as dive-bombers.

During several operations out of Singapore, the Dutch Brewsters carried out various operations, including sinking a Japanese destroyer and shooting down four Japanese aircraft.

During the defence of Singapore one Brewster pilot lost his life. On 18 January 1942 the remaining aircraft were taken back to Java to cover the Dutch shortages. Besides the Brewster fighters, some bombers from other aircraft groups of the ML-KNIL were used to defend Singapore.

Malacca was defended by the Third Indian Army Corps. This was reinforced with units from Australia.

The British reinforced the defence of the island, but they were not too diligent in this. In the words of a British non-commissioned officer:

> *"I hope we don't get too strong in Malacca, because then the Japanese won't dare make a landing at all."*

The overall atmosphere on the island was one of an unconcerned and unfounded sense of colonial superiority.

On the Japanese side not everything was rosy. The plans for the attack on Malaya were entrusted to General Yamashita. The relationship between him and his superior Tojo was distrustful and hostile.

On November 2, 1941, Yamashita received command of the 25th Army（第25軍 , *Dai-nijyūgo gun*) for the attack on Malacca and Singapore. At the same time, Masaharu Homma was given command of the 14th Army for the attack on the Philippines, and Hitoshi Imamura was given command of the 16th Army for the attack on the Dutch East Indies.

Yamashita had little time for preparation. Nevertheless, he arranged air cover by the 3rd Air Fleet with 459 aircraft and by 159 naval aircraft.

The island of Hainan, halfway between Japan and Malacca, was to serve as a base of operations. He rejected two of the five divisions offered because he concluded that the supply capacity for them was insufficient. The 25th Army would consist of the 18th

Division under General Renya Mutaguchi, the 5th Division under General Takuro Matsui, and a division of the Imperial Guard under General Takuma Nishimura.

The officers did not know each other; Yamashita's job was to forge them into a unit. However, cooperation with Nishimura would prove problematic throughout the campaign. Count General Hisaichi Terauchi, the commander of the Southern Army, had a colonel on his staff who had studied jungle warfare on Hainan. Yamashita benefited greatly from this, but also knew that Terauchi was using this colonel as a spy.

There were several thousand Japanese living in Singapore, and Yamashita had fairly reliable intelligence at his disposal. He quickly concluded that he would have to

cross not 30 bridges, but 500 bridges on his way from north to south.

On 4 December 1941, the 25th Army embarked.The coordination was very important, because the landing in Malacca had to take place almost simultaneously with the attack on Pearl Harbor, despite the long distance and the different time zones.

On 6 December 1941 an Australian reconnaissance plane observed the Japanese fleet of 25 transport ships, accompanied by a heavy cruiser, five cruisers and smaller ships.British Admiral Sir Thomas Phillips and American Admiral Thomas C. Hart concluded from the course that either neutral Thailand or Malacca was the target.

The Repulse was recalled from her trip to Darwin. Four American destroyers were sent to the area of operations. Further reconnaissance by British aircraft failed due to bad weather and Air Marshal Sir Robert Brooke-Popham decided not to launch a defensive invasion of neutral Thailand.

The fighting for Malacca

On 7 December 1941 two Japanese infantry divisions landed in Malacca. Landing at Kota Bahru, the Japanese lost between 300 and 800 men due to stiff resistance from the Indian Dogra battalion and British air raids.

In further fighting the British units proved practically powerless against the Japanese army.

Poor coordination on the British side led to a successful Japanese attack on 9 December 1941 on the airfield of Singapore, in which the RAF lost almost all of its fighter aircraft stationed in Singapore.

On 11 and 12 December 1941 the British troops suffered an ignominious defeat at the Battle of Jitra, despite the virtual absence of artillery on the Japanese side.

A raid on 8 December 1941 by the British battleships *Prince of Wales* and *Repulse* in an attempt to intercept a Japanese invasion fleet led to their sinking on 10 December 1941 in an attack by Japanese aircraft.

The British defence was simply rushed to Singapore after the battle of Jitra. Every defensive position was quickly flanked or breached by the well-trained Japanese units.

The good jungle training of the Japanese troops proved to be of great value. As the Japanese troops gained ground, they also gained control of the newly constructed airfields, which enabled them to effectively assert their air superiority.

On 11 January 1942 the Japanese took the Malaysian capital Kuala Lumpur. Yamashita had serious supply problems in the meantime, but the capture of this city solved them.

The Australian units twice managed to trap the Japanese vanguard, but were also mercilessly hunted south after this.

The fighting for Singapore

On 31 January 1942 the last British troops, demoralised, withdrew from Malacca over a stone dam connecting the island of Singapore to the mainland.

The commander of the Australian forces summed up the Allied defeat thus:

> "The whole operation sounds incredible: 550 miles pushed back in 55 days by a small Japanese army of two divisions, riding on stolen bicycles and with no artillery support."

Percival spread his men over the entire 70 km stretch of coastline of the island, stretching the defences very thin.

On 8 February 1942 Japanese troops crossed the narrow straits separating Singapore from Malacca (Johore Strait).Already 2 days later, on 10 February 1942, the British were forced to withdraw from the northern part of the island on a second defensive line.The next day, 11 February 1942, the Japanese under Tomoyuki Yamashita were already on the outskirts.

On February 13, 1942, knowing that his supplies were in serious trouble, Yamashita called on British commander Lieutenant General Arthur Percival to "cease this futile and desperate resistance."

The next day the Allies managed to hold a small area on the south side of the island, but on 14 February 1942 they lost ground again.His chief advisers advised Percival to surrender, also to minimise civilian casualties.Percival did not receive permission to surrender from Winston Churchill.

The next day the Allies fought on, the number of civilian casualties increased.One million civilians were concentrated in the small area where the Allies held on despite artillery shelling and bombing.The water supply became endangered. Japanese troops killed two hundred patients and staff members of the "Alexandra Barracks Hospital", because the British army had set up machine gun nests on the first and second floor.

On the morning of 15 February 1942, Japanese forces broke through the last British defences in the north.The Allies were now also seriously short of food and some types of ammunition.After meeting with his subordinates, Percival contacted the Japanese and shortly after 17:15 local time signed the surrender.

Some 130,000 Indian, Australian and British troops were made prisoners of war: the largest surrender of British soldiers in history.

Consequences

The Singapore fortress had been the connecting link in the American-British-Dutch-Australian Command (ABDACOM).With the fall of Singapore coordination problems arose in this command.Within weeks the Dutch East Indies fell. The strategic oil wells of the Dutch East Indies fell into Japanese hands.

The Allied command area was geographically split in two into Indian Ocean and Pacific sections. The Americans took the lead in the Pacific and Australia area, the South West Pacific Area Command, the British took over in the areas bordering the Indian Ocean, the South East Asia Command.

Japanese-occupied Singapore was renamed by them in *Syonan-to* (昭南島 *Shōnan-tō*), "Light of the South Island".

Yamashita acquired the nickname "Tiger of Malacca". He was transferred to a post on the Sino-Russian border, where he was not killed in action. On 23 February 1946 the Americans sentenced him to the noose for the war crimes committed by his men in the Philippines.

Still Anglo-Saxon sources often attribute Japan's rapid advance through Malacca and Singapore to Japanese air superiority and Japanese tank superiority.These defenses, however, on closer analysis prove a weak excuse. The Japanese troops did not have tanks or artillery, certainly not at first. However, they were experienced and trained in jungle warfare.The British at the beginning had the airfields, aircraft, two battleships, and sufficient supplies. The Japanese operated 500 miles from their nearest base.

By the speed with which Yamashita managed to advance, he deprived the British of the opportunity to occupy good positions and strengthen them sufficiently. He managed to minimize his weaknesses and took full advantage of the British weaknesses.

The battle is considered one of the greatest defeats of British forces in history.

After the Japanese capture of Penang, the advance towards Singapore began. The city was called "the strongest naval port in the east" by Churchill, and no Briton expected the port to fall to the Japanese. The defense of Singapore was mainly against a landing from the sea, not against an attack through Malacca, and that was exactly what the Japanese did: During their advance amphibious transports kept getting behind the British lines, forcing them to retreat. From Kota Bharu a second Japanese unit simultaneously headed south along the inland railway. On 29 December 1941 the Japanese rallied around Johoro from three different directions.

Earlier, on 10 December 1941, the modern British battleships HMS Repulse and HMS Prince of Wales had already been sunk by Japanese aircraft, greatly reducing Singapore's naval defense against a landing.In Singapore, it was believed that the city was well defended and would never be attacked. The city had a defense force of 85,000 men and an air force of 141 obsolete aircraft. Yet on 8 December 1941 a Japanese air raid was launched on Singapore. Singapore resisted for over two weeks as the Japanese crossed Jehore Strait, but on 15 February 1942 Singapore capitulated to the Japanese, a heavy defeat for the British.

In January 1942 the Japanese invaded the British colony of Burma (Myanmar). Rangoon fell in March. With reinforcements of allied Thai troops and Japanese troops that became available after the capture of Singapore, the Japanese were able to take most of Burma within a few months. A chaotic withdrawal of British and Chinese defenders to India and China followed. The Japanese began building a railway from Bangkok to Rangoon in 1943 to bring troops in for an invasion of India. This *Death Railway* was the inspiration for the movie *The Bridge on the River Kwai.*

Conquest of the Dutch East Indies

The Dutch East Indies (Indonesia) were rich in oil and therefore occupied a vital place for Japan during the Second World War. Earlier attempts had been made through political consultation to bring Indonesia into the Japanese sphere of influence, but the United States was strongly opposed and threatened to impose all kinds of sanctions.

Because of the German invasion of the Netherlands and the limited room for manoeuvre of the government in London, the Dutch East Indies was not in the best state of defence. In addition, large parts of the navy and air force were under British or Australian command in places like Singapore, because those places were considered of greater strategic importance than the Dutch East Indies. In total the defense of Indonesia (East Indies) consisted of 30000 men of the Royal Dutch-Indies Army (KNIL), native police soldiers of the "Landstorm", 79 bombers (and later ten Australian) and the Royal Navy, including the light cruiser Tromp.

The Japanese attacks on the Dutch East Indies began on 10 January 1942 when Japanese troops landed around Tarakan on Borneo.The Japanese landed on the east coast of the island, which was only weakly occupied by Dutch troops. At the same time, the Japanese made landings on Celebes, near the town of Manado, which was important because of its sheltered bay and base for seaplanes.On 11 January 1942, the Japanese made their largest landing and captured Manado.

Invasion of Sumatra in 1942

After the Japanese attack on Pearl Harbor, the Netherlands had declared war on Japan the following day. Because of the presence of raw materials the Dutch East Indies were an attractive target for Japan. The war began with the Japanese landing on Borneo on December 17, 1941. However, it was clear that other islands would soon follow.

From early 1942 preparations for the defence began. In Aceh and East Coast (North Sumatra) the Territorial Command had been in the hands of Colonel Vic Gosenson since 1936. In early February Major-General Roelof Overakker was transferred from East Java to Central Sumatra where he took charge of the military command. On South Sumatra lieutenant-colonel L.N.W. Vogelsang was in charge.

The defence of Sumatra - like everywhere else in the archipelago - was poorly organised. It was clear that they stood little chance against the Japanese army. Because of budget cuts the Royal Dutch East Indies Army (KNIL) had few modern weapons at its disposal. Shortly before the outbreak of war so-called *destruction parties* were organised. These were Indonesian civilians whose task was to destroy important bridges, roads, oil refineries and other support points before they fell into the hands of the Japanese. Because a large number of VPs were prematurely transferred to Java, because fighting had also broken out there, they could do little on Sumatra.

Battle of Palembang

The battle for Sumatra began with the Battle of Palembang. Palembang was a strategically important place because of the presence of an oil refinery. The Allied forces had centred their air defense there around two airfields. The Royal Australian Air Force stationed 40 Bristol Blenheim bombers and 35 Lockheed Hudsons on the island. Other aircraft from the British, Australian and New Zealand air forces followed later. The KNIL had about two thousand men stationed around the airfields.

The first Japanese air raids took place on February 6. On the morning of 13 February, the British ship *HMS Li Wo*, commanded by Lieutenant Thomas Wilkinson, encountered the Japanese invasion convoy. Despite its light armament, the ship opened the attack and put one of the Japanese transport ships into lighter fire, while several others were damaged. When the ammunition ran out after 90 minutes, Wilkinson gave the order to ram the nearest transport ship before his own ship was destroyed by Japanese fire.

While Allied aircraft attacked the Japanese invasion fleet, on February 13, the Japanese air force dropped a few hundred paratroopers. One hundred and eighty Japanese landed between Palembang and Pangkalan Benteng and more than 90 west of the oil refinery in Pladju. Two hours after the first landing, another 60 paratroopers were dropped near the airfield. They failed to take the airfield, but the oil refinery fell into their hands undamaged. A hasty counterattack by members of the Landstorm and anti-aircraft troops was successful to the extent that the complex was retaken. Little came of the previously planned destruction of the refinery in case of a Japanese attack.

From ABDACOM, the joint Allied command structure, all Allied aircraft were ordered to divert to Java, where a major Japanese attack was expected. Other military personnel were evacuated via Oosthaven in the direction of Java or the British East Indies. This meant the actual fall of Palembang.

Battle in Central and North Sumatra

In Central Sumatra Major-General Overakker, who had about 2,500 to 3,000 KNIL soldiers at his disposal, thought he had too few men to defend both the east and west coasts of the island. He therefore decided to concentrate his troops on the west coast and then slowly withdraw to Emmahaven and Pedang to defend the harbours there. Gosenson on North Sumatra had only about a thousand soldiers at his disposal.

Events beyond the control of the Dutch on Sumatra determined their fate. During the various naval battles most of the Allied fleet was destroyed.

On Java, the most important island of the archipelago, the KNIL was overrun by the Japanese. On March 9 they surrendered under the command of Lieutenant-General Hein ter Poorten. On Sumatra Major-General Overakker and Colonel Gosenson had agreed beforehand to continue fighting in case of capitulation. The plan was to withdraw to the Alas Valley, a rugged mountainous area near Blangkedjeren, and to start a guerrilla war from there.

Especially in Aceh the Dutch had made many enemies, including during the Aceh War. The Japanese major Fujiwari Iwaiwchi had founded a nationalist organisation in Malacca in December 1941, which now actively opposed the Dutch.

Moreover, the troops coming from the south had to travel long distances. Therefore few KNIL soldiers managed to reach the valley.

The first Japanese, members of the 25th Army, set foot on North Sumatra on March 12. In total there were about ten thousand men. They quickly captured large parts of the northeast coast and then moved inland.

The Japanese forces could also count on air support. It was therefore soon clear to Gosenson and Overakker that their mission had no chance of success. They surrendered near Kutatjane on 28 March, leaving Sumatra entirely in Japanese hands.

Battle of borneo

Borneo was an attractive target. It was weakly defended and offered many opportunities for oil extraction. Petroleum was crucial for Japan to sustain the war in the long term.

Furthermore, the capture of Borneo was necessary to control important sea routes to islands such as Java, Sumatra and Celebes.

Allied forces united into a joint command structure under the name ABDACOM (American-British-Dutch-Australian Command) in December 1941. Air Marshal Robert Brooke-Popham had shipped several army units to Borneo at the end of 1940. These were mainly stationed around Kuching. The total army strength was about 1050 men. The White Rajah government had raised another 1500 or so men organized as the Sarawak Rangers.

The Dutch forces had centred themselves around Singkawang II airfield, which was near the border with Sarawak. That airfield was defended by more than 700 men. Five Brewster F2A fighters and ten Martin B-10 bombers arrived on 25 November. The Naval Air Service had a base at Pontianak, with three Dornier Do 24 flying boats and protected by a KNIL garrison, consisting of almost 500 soldiers and commanded by Lieutenant Colonel Dominicus Mars.

Fights

The main force of the Japanese invasion force, commanded by Major General Kiyotake Kawachguchi, was formed by the 35th Infantry Brigade. It left Cam Ranh Bay in French Indochina on 13 December and consisted of ten transport ships. She was escorted by a cruiser, four torpedo boats and a submarine. The support group consisted of two cruisers and two torpedo boats. The first targets were Miri and Seria, two cities on the north coast of Borneo with large oil fields nearby.

Immediately after the attack on Pearl Harbor the British had already proceeded to destroy the ollie winning installations, just in time as the Japanese arrived a week later and took both places with little resistance. Another target was Kuching and the nearby airfields. However, the convoy there was discovered and attacked by the Dutch Martin B-10 bombers, but with little damage. More successful were the three Dornier Do 24 flying boats that followed, although one was shot down. Another flying boat placed a direct hit and sank the torpedo boat *Shinonome*. Both remaining flying boats still attacked the Japanese at Miri on 18 and 19 December, but then withdrew to Sumatra as the Japanese had discovered Sinkawang II airfield and immediately proceeded to attack.

A Japanese convoy left Miri for Kuching on 22 December, but was discovered by a Dutch flying boat. The Dutch submarine *H.M. K XIV* infiltrated the convoy on the night of December 23 and sank two transport ships, killing hundreds of Japanese. However, most of the force did arrive in Kuching and the British present there were overrun and had to abandon the city. The survivors of the 15th Punjab Regiment retreated to Sinkawang

The next night another Dutch submarine, the *Hr.Ms. K XVI,* managed to sink the Japanese torpedo boat *Sagiri* 50 kilometres north of Kuching. On 25 December, the K XVI was in turn chased to the bottom of the sea by a Japanese submarine. All 36 crew members lost their lives. On 24 and 28 December B-10 bombers bombed the Japanese in Kuching from Singapore. On 26 December Allied bombers sank a minesweeper and a freighter.

Meanwhile, on 31 December 1941, a Japanese force moved further north to also capture Brunei, Labuan and Jesselton (now known as Kota Kinabalu). On 18 January 1942 the Japanese landed in small fishing boats near Sandakan, the government centre of North Borneo. Although the British had a force of just under 650 men, there was hardly any resistance and the British governor Charles Robert Smith surrendered.

Sinkawang had also fallen on 29 December, after which the remaining Dutch and British troops withdrew into the jungle and moved south to Sampit and Pangkalanbun. Meanwhile South and Central Kalimantan were under attack by Japan from the west and east. On 29 January 1942 Pontianak fell as the last major town in Borneo. The last Allied troops that had retreated into the jungle surrendered on 1 April 1942.

In the days that followed the Japanese launched attacks on places in the Dutch East Indies where oil was being produced or which were of strategic importance, such as Balikpapan and Pemangkat (Borneo) and Kendari (Celebes).On 29 January a joint Australian/Dutch force was defeated on Ambon and Australia came within range of the Japanese planes.Heavy fighting took place around the town of Palembang in southern Sumatra, where not only oil but also two refineries were located.

Dutch Timor, together with Portuguese Timor, was attacked by Australian troops on 12 December 1942.

The weak defences were no match for the superiorly armed Japanese and Timor surrendered. An attempt to prevent a Japanese landing on Java failed and on 28 February 1942 Japanese troops landed at Eretan Wetan, nerve centre of the Dutch East Indies. The battle lasted more than a week, and the decision by the Dutch to defend only the more strategically and economically important West Java delayed the Japanese advance considerably. Nevertheless, the defeated KNIL was unable to prevent Java from falling into the hands of the conquerors.

By the end of February, the Japanese controlled most of Dutch Timor and the area around Dili in the northeast. However, they could not move to the south and east of the island without fear of attack. The 2/2nd (independent company) was hidden in the mountains of Portuguese

Timor and began attacks against the Japanese, supported by Timorese guides and porters with Timorese mountain ponies.

Although Portuguese officials remained officially neutral and responsible for civil affairs, the colonists and Portuguese Timorese were mostly sympathetic to the Allies, enabling them to use the local telephone system to communicate among themselves and to gather information about Japanese movements. However, they were unable to contact the outside world, which was due to a lack of functioning radio equipment.

The Japanese offensive

In August, Japanese forces had begun burning down villages that would have provided aid to the Allies. The commander of the Japanese 48th Division, Lieutenant General Yuichi Tsuchihashi had arrived to take charge of operations on Timor. He moved troops to the east of Dutch Timor to attack the Dutch positions in the central south of the island. The offensive ended on 19 August, after capturing the central town of Maubisse and the southern port of Beco.

In late August, matters were complicated when a rebellion against the Portuguese broke out among the natives, starting a parallel conflict. The Japanese were also recruiting large numbers of Timorese civilians as scouts to observe and pass on Allied movements.

In September, the main body of Japan's 48th Division arrived to take over the campaign. The Australians also sent reinforcements on 23 September, in the form of the 450-strong 2/4th Independent Company - known as Lancer Force. The destroyer *HMAS Voyager* ran aground in the southern port of Betano during the landing of the 2/4th.

By October the Japanese had succeeded in recruiting significant numbers of Timorese civilians to join the fight, these however suffered severe losses in frontal attacks against the Allies. The colonists were also pressured to help the Japanese, and at least 26 Portuguese civilians were killed in the first six months of the occupation, including local officials and a Catholic priest. On November 1, the Allied Supreme Command approved the issue of arms to Portuguese officials.

On December 11-12, the rest of the original *Sparrow Force*, with the exception of a few officers, was evacuated with a number of Portuguese civilians, by the Dutch destroyer *Hr.Ms. Tjerk Hiddes.*

By this time there was little chance of an Allied Timor, for there were now 12,000 Japanese troops on the island, and the commandos were increasingly in contact with the enemy.

The Japanese also landed on Dutch New Guinea near Hollandia and started to advance towards the Australian part. On 23 January 1942 the Japanese occupied the port of Rabaul without meeting much resistance. This harbour was one of the best natural harbours in the world and the key to controlling the Bismarck Archipelago. It was quickly captured from the demoralised Allied troops.

On New Guinea itself the battle got tougher and tougher: the Japanese encountered heavy resistance for the first time in their war of conquest. On the 8th of March the Japanese managed to occupy the towns of Lae and Salamaua with little effort, by which they controlled all of northern New Guinea. A supply route, the Kokoda Trail, a mountain pass through the jungle over the Owen Stanley Mountains, was the Allies' only lifeline.

At the same time a Japanese corps landed on the Solomon Islands east of New Guinea, and the British troops there had to capitulate. This was the end of the Japanese expansion: they failed to capture southern Dutch New Guinea and the defended islands between the Solomon Islands and New Guinea.

Turning point of the war

Guam and Wake were of great strategic and military importance in the Pacific. America had a naval and air base there, and could thus cover much of the central Pacific with bombers, a serious threat to advanced Japanese positions around the Gilbert Islands and Marshall Islands.

Guam was attacked by overwhelming Japanese forces, and after only two days had to cease its resistance against the enemy that surrounded it everywhere.Wake managed to withstand the first weak Japanese landing, and the planes of Wake islands carried out a few more flights over the Mariana Islands, but then came seven torpedo boats that launched a bombardment after which a stronger Japanese squadron landed.This time Wake did have to capitulate to the more powerful enemy.

After the successful attack on Pearl Harbor, Japan wanted a foothold in the central Pacific. An invasion of Hawaii was ruled out for the time being, despite the success of 7 December 1941. Midway, almost halfway the Tokyo-Hawaii line, was an excellent alternative. Early in June

1942 a huge Japanese fleet sailed out to capture the small archipelago with its great strategic value. At the same time a fleet sailed out to conquer the Aleutians. But the Americans had cracked the Japanese secret code and were ready with fighters and bombers from the airfield at Midway and the three remaining carriers *Enterprise*, *Hornet* and *Yorktown*.

On June 5th 1942 the Battle of Midway took place. The Americans surprised the Japanese completely. American Admiral Nimitz nevertheless needed a fair amount of luck to repel the Japanese attack. The Japanese aircraft carriers were attacked while their decks happened to be full of fully fueled planes and bombs. Six hits were enough to destroy two Japanese carriers. Later in the day, the Americans sunk two more carriers. The Japanese then called off the invasion of Midway. The Japanese did manage to bomb Midway themselves with bombers that had taken off from their carriers earlier that day.

The American victory at Midway was the first time the Allies succeeded in stopping Japan. Midway marked the turning point of the war in the Pacific. In the meantime the Japanese managed to annex a number of islands in the

Aleutians, but these were gradually recaptured after the Japanese mistaken withdrawal at the Battle of the Komandorski Islands.

The Japanese did not give up and launched an attack on the Solomon Islands, a series of islands northeast of Australia. Knowing the Japanese radio codes, the Americans knew about the invasion and sent a large fleet to repel it. The two fleets collided in the Coral Sea in May 1942, defeating the Japanese.

The Battle of the Coral Sea

The Battle of the Coral Sea, early May 1942, can in several ways be seen as a turning point in World War II.It was the first naval battle in which aircraft carriers attacked each other and the first naval battle in which neither ship saw the other. It also marked the point at which the Japanese advance in the Pacific was halted for the first time.

Background

Having overrun large parts of Southeast Asia in a few months, the Japanese Empire was at the height of its military power. The Allies were still reeling from a series of defeats. They were trying to scrape together the equipment and skills needed to survive and to one day strike back.Allied strategy focused on a defensive buildup of U.S. Army and Marine Corps forces on New Caledonia and Australian air and ground forces at Port Moresby in southern New Guinea.

In April 1942, Japanese forces departed from their support base at Rabaul for a double amphibious invasion at Port Moresby (Operation MO), and Tulagi in the Solomon Islands.

The objective was threefold: gain control of the Solomon Islands, capture Port Moresby (the last base between Japan and the Australian continent), and force the American aircraft carriers into combat for the first time in the war.

Historians are divided on the Japanese long-term goal. There seems little doubt that they saw the Solomon Islands as a bastion against future American counterattacks. It also seems plausible, that they had an invasion of northern Australia in mind.

However, there is considerable doubt about Japanese longer-term goals. The practice of Japanese planning was complex, with ill-defined areas of responsibility, and bitter debates between army and navy.

Several fleets sailed: the invasion forces for the Solomon Islands and Port Moresby, and a protection fleet consisting of two new, large aircraft carriers (*Shokaku* and *Zuikaku*, both veterans of the Attack on Pearl Harbor), a smaller aircraft carrier (*Shoho*), two heavy cruisers, and support aircraft.

By overhearing radio messages, the Allies knew that the Japanese aircraft stationed ashore were being moved south and that a major operation was imminent.

They were able to counter this with three fleets: USS *Yorktown* (CV-5) already in the Coral Sea under the command of Admiral Frank Jack Fletcher, USS *Lexington* (CV-2) en route here, and a fleet of surface ships.The aircraft carriers USS *Hornet* (CV-8) and USS *Enterprise* (CV-6) were heading south after the Doolittle Raid on Tokyo but arrived too late to join the battle.

The battle

1-6 May

The *Lexington* arrived at the *Yorktown* on May 1. The Japanese occupied Tulagi without opposition on 3 May, and began construction of an airfield. After taking fuel, the *Yorktown* steamed toward Tulagi and made several successful attacks on Japanese ships and aircraft on 4 May. As a result, the Americans betrayed the presence of their aircraft carrier, but sunk the Japanese destroyer *Mikazuki*.

The ability of the airfield to conduct reconnaissance flights from the island was damaged. After this the *Yorktown* withdrew to the agreed rendezvous point with the *Lexington* and the newly arrived cruisers.

Meanwhile, two large Japanese aircraft carriers approached from the south, trapping the American fleet between two Japanese fleets.

Land-based B-17s attacked the Port Moresby approaching invasion fleet on 6 May, but to no avail. (It would be almost another year before it was recognized that high-flying bombing flights on moving ships were aimless.)

Although both fleets made many reconnaissance flights on 6 May, they were unable to locate each other on that day, partly due to cloud cover.

During the night the two fleets were more than 100 km apart. Other Allied aircraft joined the battle from air bases at Cooktown and Iron Range on the Cape York Peninsula.

6-7 May

That night Fletcher made the difficult decision to send away his main surface ships under the command of Australian Admiral John Crace to block the most likely course of the Japanese invasion fleet to Port Moresby. Crace's fleet consisted of the cruisers HMAS *Australia*, USS *Chicago* (CA-29), HMAS *Hobart,* and the destroyers USS *Perkins*, USS *Walke*, and USS *Farragut*.Both Fletcher and Crace realized the risk, that with this squadron, with no air protection exposed to the attacks of land-based Japanese aircraft, risked suffering the same fate as the British battleships HMS *Prince of Wales* and HMS *Repulse* five months earlier.

Their fears were realized when the squadron was spotted by a squadron of Japanese torpedo bombers in the afternoon of May 7 and suffered a number of intense air attacks.

By luck or skill, the Allied ships escaped, losing *USS Neosho (AO-23)* and *USS Sims*. A few minutes after the Japanese attack, the squadron was mistakenly attacked by American B-17s. Again the *Farragut* and *Perkins escaped* without damage.

American reconnaissance aircraft spotted the Japanese invasion fleet with the small Japanese carrier *Shoho*. This was mistaken for the main Japanese fleet, and Fletcher deployed 53 bombers, 22 torpedo planes, and 18 fighters for an attack. The *Shoho* was sunk in this attack.

8 May

On the morning of May 8, the Japanese had the advantage. A low cloud cover hung over their carriers, which would make searching for Allied planes difficult. Fletcher's carriers sailed under cloudless skies.

Nevertheless, the reconnaissance planes of both sides found each other's fleets in fairly quick succession. Immediately afterwards, both forces launched air attacks on the carriers of the other side. Hidden in the rain, the *Zuikaku* escaped reconnaissance, but the *Shokaku* was hit by three bombs. On fire, the *Shokaku was* unable to board her returning aircraft. She was put out of action.

Both American aircraft carriers were hit in the Japanese attack: the *Yorktown* by a bomb, the larger and less maneuverable *Lexington* by both bombs and torpedoes. She survived the initial damage, and it was assessed as repairable. An hour later, however, jet fuel exploded and the ship had to be abandoned and torpedoed to avoid falling into Japanese hands.

Crace's force remained in position between the Japanese invasion fleet and Port Moresby. Inoue, misled by erroneous aircraft reports on the strength of the Allied squadron, ordered the invasion force to turn back.

Historical impact

- In tactical terms the Japanese gained a marginal victory: they lost a small aircraft carrier and the Americans lost a large one. Both still had heavy damage to one of their large carriers, but for the Allies it was a boost: after five months of continuous defeats, there was finally a battle in which they struck on equal terms.
- The boost to morale was extremely important: it gave the Americans confidence that they could defeat Japan.
- Landing from the sea at Port Moresby was prevented. Moresby formed a vital point in Allied strategy, and could not yet be defended by the ground forces stationed there. The loss of Port

Moresby would almost certainly have meant an invasion into, and possibly even the loss of, Australia.

- As a result of the averted landing from the sea, Japan was forced to attempt to take Port Moresby by land. This delay was just enough to allow the arrival of the experienced *Second Australian Imperial Force*. These subsequently fought in the Kokoda Track campaign and the Battle of Milne Bay. This relieved the pressure on Guadalcanal.
- Without a base in New Guinea the Allied advance in the Pacific would have been more costly and protracted than it is now.
- The loss of the *USS Lexington* was a serious blow, but the Americans were able to absorb losses faster than Japan.
- The United States Navy learned much from this battle. From the loss of the *Lexington,* the Navy learned better ways to store aviation fuel on aircraft carriers. It also improved the control of the defensive aircraft screen around the aircraft carriers. From the attacks on the Japanese carriers, valuable lessons about the coordination of dive bombers and torpedo bombers (too late for

the Battle of Midway, but useful for the longer term) followed.

- The *USS Yorktown* returned to Pearl Harbor.
- Although it was estimated that the repair of the *Yorktown* would take months, the crews in Pearl Harbor performed a top performance by getting her seaworthy again in a very short time. She was therefore present again during the most important Battle of Midway. This presence proved decisive (three aircraft carriers instead of two).
- Because the *Shokaku* was damaged and the *Zuikaku* was short of aircraft, neither were able to participate in the crucial Battle of Midway a month later.
- Although the *Zuikaku* was only slightly damaged, and she still carried 40 aircraft, she had to return to Japan for repairs. *Shokaku*'s repair took six months. Neither was present at the Battle of Midway. The absence of *Zuikaku* and *Shokaku* at Midway was fatal for Japan as it turned out afterwards: two less aircraft carriers on the Japanese side.
- Japan could still make up for the loss of aircraft and even aircraft carriers, but would never make

up for the loss of its most experienced and trained pilots.

The Battle of Guadalcanal

The **Battle of Guadalcanal**, also known by the code name **Operation Watchtower**, during World War II led to the capture by American forces of the Japanese-occupied island of Guadalcanal (part of the British Solomon Islands in the Pacific Ocean) in 1942.

There were 24,000 Japanese casualties and 6,000 American casualties - limited numbers compared to other battles. The campaign was marked by grim fighting and a number of firsts:

- first defeat of the Japanese land forces
- the first amphibious landing of US forces since 1898
- variety of battles (fleet actions, coastal bombardments, guerrilla tactics, land warfare, air combat)

Introduction

Guadalcanal lies in the middle of the elongated chain of Solomon Islands north of Australia.

The Imperial Japanese Navy wanted to turn the Solomon Islands into a major strategic base and in 1942 began a program to occupy all the islands and build airfields here for land-based patrol bombers.

Guadalcanal would become the main base in the middle of the chain. If they succeeded, Allied shipping between the US and Australia would have to make a long detour along the south. Japan already had a base at Rabaul, in the north of the island chain.

Again and again the opponents brought in reinforcements, nobody wanted to think about losing this battle. The Japanese occupied Guadalcanal in July 1942, as a way station on their way to Australia and Hawaii; the Americans (more specifically Admiral Ernest King, head of the operation) wanted to use it as a base for their advance in a north-westerly direction. Admiral Isoroku Yamamoto, commander of the Japanese fleet, did not realize at the outset the importance of this confrontation and the resources it would require.

The loss of Guadalcanal meant that the Japanese were in a defensive position and the Americans could use the island as a springboard for the advance on Japan.

Operation Watchtower

General Alexander Vandegrift was appointed commander of American ground forces barely five weeks before the attack began in a battle that would eventually lead to the evacuation of the island by the Japanese. The period between August 1942 and February 1943 saw a number of land, sea, and air confrontations that are described in detail below.

- the landing on August 7, 1942
- Naval battle off Savo Island on August 9, 1942, a first unsuccessful attempt by the Japanese Navy to drive out the Americans, despite their heavy losses.
- On 18 August Colonel Kiyono Ichiki landed on the island with 950 men. During a threefold banzai attack of these elite troops more than 700 Japanese were killed. Colonel Ichiki committed harakiri.

- In the naval battle off the Eastern Solomon Islands on 24 August, the American aircraft carrier *USS Enterprise (CV-6)* was badly damaged. The Japanese also lost their aircraft carrier Ryujo.
- On 12-14 September, Colonel Mike Edson repulsed an attack by 7,000 Japanese led by Major General Kiyotake Kawaguchi. This confrontation was later called the *Battle of Bloody Ridge*. Heavy aerial bombardment of Henderson Field and artillery shelling preceded it.
- On 15 September, the aircraft carrier *Wasp* was lost in a submarine attack. The heavy cruiser *North Carolina* took a torpedo hit. 4,000 American soldiers aboard transport ships landed safely.
- Lieutenant General Haruyoshi Hyakutake landed 20,000 men on October 9. Vandergrift saw his force strengthened by 4,000 soldiers.
- The Naval Battle of Cape Esperance on 11-12 October ended with a slight American advantage. However, the U.S. Navy was able to delay but not prevent the continuous landings of Japanese troops (affectionately referred to by the Marines as the *Tokyo Express*).

- On 13 October Henderson Field was again shelled by naval artillery and by *Pistol Pete* (a piece of heavy field artillery). In eighty minutes 918 heavy caliber shells hit the airfield rendering it unusable.
- Hyakutake made new plans to launch a three-pronged attack from different directions on Henderson Field on 18 October. The Japanese navy and air force provided support. Difficulties in transporting guns through the jungle and unrelenting rain caused a delay until October 24. Units under the command of General Sumioyosji, unaware of the postponement, launched their attack on 23 October. 650 Japanese were killed. The attack of the Sendaidivision was repulsed the next day (more than 900 Japanese killed). Marine artillery, bombers and *Pistol Pete* shelled American positions on 25 October (dug-out sunday). In the evening Japanese ground troops attacked again; again without success. From 29 October they began to withdraw.
- In the night of 25 to 26 October a new confrontation between the Japanese and American navies took place (Battle of the Santa Cruz Islands). The Americans lost the aircraft carrier

Hornet, the destroyer *Porter* and 74 aircraft. The aircraft carrier *Enterprise* and the *South Dakota* were damaged. The Japanese lost 100 aircraft. Their aircraft carriers *Shokaku* and *Zuiho*, the heavy cruiser *Chikuma*, and the destroyer *Terutsuki* were heavily damaged.

Counter-offensive of the Allies

Now the Allies had the advantage of being able to choose where the next attack would be, but there was a duel in the Allied camp. The US wanted a direct attack on Micronesia to push on to Japan itself. After the conquest of Micronesia, they wanted to advance to the Marianas, then Okinawa and then via an armada of ships and planes to Japan itself. The other Allies first wanted to eliminate the threat to their own borders by first freeing Southeast Asia from the Japanese. It was decided to implement both strategies: the British began the reconquest of Burma, the Chinese entered Japanese-China, and the Americans advanced to Micronesia.

The resistance of the Japanese was very strong, and they fought for every yard of ground.Micronesia was conquered, and then also Burma and parts of eastern China.The Allies were getting closer and closer to Japan, and the resistance of the Japanese was less and less, the fleet and air force suffered heavy losses, and the Japanese pilots instituted their kamikaze tactics, plunging their planes straight into the Allied ships.

When Guam was finally retaken in August 1944, heavy B-29 bombers were able to attack Japan from the island, and a long series of bomb attacks on Japanese cities began, destroying the country's entire infrastructure, although it did not break the morale of the Japanese as expected.

In February 1945 the Americans landed on Iwo Jima with the aim of capturing the two airfields on the island. After heavy fighting, Iwo Jima was taken a month later. In April the Americans landed on the island of Okinawa, directly south of the Japanese main islands. A terrible battle ensued, in which the Japanese pulled out all the stops to hold the island, including kamikaze on a large scale. After bitter fighting the last Japanese surrendered on June 23rd.

The landing on Iwo Jima

The Landing on Iwo Jima (codenamed Operation Detachment) was an American landing operation on the island of Iwo Jima in February 1945 that was part of the fighting in the Pacific Ocean between the United States and Imperial Japan during World War II.

The Americans wanted to use Iwo Jima as a base for their (air)attacks on Japan. They managed to conquer the island from the Japanese and gained control over the three airfields there, the only one between Japan and the Mariana Islands and 1250 km from Tokyo. The Japanese had used these to intercept American bombers on their way to and from their bombing raids on Japan and now the Americans could use the island as a base for attacks on mainland Japan.

Predict

At the time of the attack on Pearl Harbor, the Japanese army had a garrison of 3700-3800 men stationed on Chichi-jima, in addition to 1200 naval personnel. This consisted of a seaplane base, a radio and weather station and several light craft like minesweepers, submarines and patrol boats.

On Iwo Jima, the Navy had built an airfield 1.5 to 2 km from Mount Suribachi. 1,500 naval aviation personnel and twenty aircraft made up the airfield's staff.

After the loss of the Marshall Islands and the devastating air attacks on Truk in the Carolinas in February 1944, Japanese military leaders reconsidered the situation. All intelligence indicated a coming American attack towards the Mariana Islands and the Carolinas. As a measure against this, they formed an inner defense line extending from the Carolinas to the Marianas, and from there to the Bonin Islands. In March 1944 the 31st Japanese Army was formed under the command of General Hideyoshi Obata to man this inner defense line.The commander of the Chichi-jima garrison became nominal commander of the army and naval units in the Bonin Islands.

Because Japan realized after the loss of the Mariana Islands in the summer of 1944 that the loss of the Bonin Islands would mean intensified bombing of the Japanese homeland, both naval and army reinforcements were sent to Iwo Jima. In March and April 1944, five hundred naval and five hundred army reinforcements arrived.Together with reinforcements from Chichi-jima and the home islands, the strength of the defense grew to five thousand men with thirteen pieces of artillery and two hundred light and heavy machine guns. The defense also had twelve heavy anti-aircraft guns, 120 mm anti-ship guns, and thirty 25 mm double-barrel anti-aircraft guns.

Japanese defense plans were complicated by the fact that after the devastating defeat of its fleet in the Battle of the Gulf of Leyte, the Navy was no longer able to effectively hinder the landings. Moreover, the air losses were so heavy that, not counting even delays from air raids, it would be until March or April 1945 before the Japanese would regain three thousand aircraft. Even then these planes could not be deployed over Iwo Jima, because the island was out of range of the Japanese planes. And what planes there were were badly needed on Formosa and the adjoining islands, where at least sufficient air bases were available.

In a postwar study, Japanese staff officers described the strategy in defending Iwo Jima as follows:

In light of the above situation, recognizing that it was impossible to conduct air, land, or sea operations that would lead to ultimate victory, it was decided that in order to gain time to prepare for the defense of the (Japanese) homeland, our forces should rely exclusively on the available defenses of the area and the objective was the slowing of the enemy advance.

It was a terrifying thought that even suicide attacks by small groups of naval and army aircraft, surprise attacks by submarines, and landings by paratroopers would be unable to exploit occasional strategic opportunities.

Even before the fall of Saipan in June 1944, the Japanese knew that Iwo Jima had to be reinforced. In late May, General Hideki Tojo informed Lieutenant General Tadamichi Kuribayashi at the Prime Minister's Office that he had been chosen to defend Iwo Jima to the end. Kuribayashi was stressed the importance of this assignment: the eyes of all Japan were on him. On June 8, Kuribayashi set out for what would be his last assignment.

In the early days of 1945, Japan faced the prospect of an Allied invasion. Daily bombing raids from the Mariana

Islands, part of Operation Scavenger, caused devastating damage. Iwo Jima served as a warning station. The arrival of American bombers was announced to Japan by radio. The Japanese air defences were ready when the Allied bombers arrived.

The landing was planned by the Allies because between the landing on Leyte in the Philippines and the landing on Okinawa there was a two-month gap in the schedule. This was not considered acceptable.

Japanese preparations

General Kuribayashi arrived on Iwo Jima between June 8 and 10 1944. At his arrival there were eighty fighter planes present, but at the beginning of July only four were left. For two days an American naval unit shelled the island from nearby. Not a building remained intact. The last four planes were also destroyed.

To the surprise of the garrison, no invasion followed in the summer of 1944. There was little doubt, however, that the Americans would launch an invasion. It was clear that in the absence of air and naval support the fall of the island was inevitable, but General Kuribayashi was determined to make the adversary pay the highest possible price. As a first step, he ordered all civilians evacuated, something that was completed by the end of July.

Kuribayashi's predecessor, Lieutenant General Hideyoshi Obata, had, in accordance with prevailing doctrine that invasions should be stopped directly on the waterfront, fortified the coastline with bunkers and artillery.General Kuribayashi held a different view. Instead of a futile attempt to hold the beaches, he had them defended with light weapons only. All artillery, mortars and rockets were placed at the base and slopes of the volcano Suribachi and on the high ground to the north.

An elaborate and well thought-out system of tunnels on different levels would be necessary for a long-term defense of the island, for the coastal bombardment had shown that buildings could not withstand the shelling of ships' guns.Engineers from Japan were brought in to design the tunnels and caves in such a way that fresh air would be present even during prolonged shelling.

At the same time, reinforcements began to arrive on the island. Kuribayashi decided to transfer the 2nd mixed brigade of five thousand men from Chichi to Iwo. After the fall of Saipan, 2,700 men of the 145th Infantry Regiment under Colonel Masuo Ikeda were transferred to Iwo Jima. In July and August these reinforcements brought the strength up to 12,700 men and an engineer battalion of 1233 men began the construction of bunkers and other fortifications.

On 10 August, Admiral Toshinosuka Ichimaru arrived, followed shortly thereafter by 2,216 naval personnel. Artillery units and five anti-tank battalions then arrived. Although many supply ships were sunk by American submarines and aircraft en route to Iwo Jima, much equipment reached the island during the summer and fall of 1944.

By the end of 1944 Kuribayashi had 361 pieces of artillery of 75 mm or heavier available. In addition to this he had a dozen 320 mm mortars, 65 medium (150 mm) and light (81 mm) mortars, 33 pieces of 80 mm marine artillery, and 94 anti-aircraft guns of 75 mm or heavier. In addition there were two hundred 20 and 25 mm anti-aircraft guns, and 69 anti-tank guns. The firepower of this artillery was augmented by seventy rocket launchers of various sizes, including a giant specimen weighing over five hundred pounds with a range of seven miles.

The 26th tank regiment was torpedoed on its way to Iwo Jima and lost all its 28 tanks. New tanks were ordered in Japan and 22 arrived in December. Colonel Nishi's intention was to deploy his tanks wherever the situation threatened to get out of hand. The hilly nature of the island prevented such use and the tanks were dug in.

All artillery was built by the Japanese in solid concrete bunkers. The Japanese found that the black volcanic ash could be turned into concrete of excellent quality. The bunkers near the beach all had a wall thickness of one meter. An extensive network of underground passages, bunkers and fortifications offered the Japanese troops excellent shelter from air raids and ship shelling. Extensive attention was paid to ventilation (the volcanic nature of the island produced a lot of sulphurous gas) and to multiple exits, so that after an air raid the crew of a bunker would not be trapped.

General Kuribayashi established his command base on the northern part of the island. His command bunkers were more than twenty meters underground, connected by two hundred meter long tunnels. Above ground, in a solid concrete bunker, seventy telegraph operators worked in shifts.

Hill 382 was the highest point on the island after the volcano. A weather station and a radio station were built here. Colonel Chosaku Kaido was in charge of all artillery on the island and had his command close to the radio station.

The largest project was a 27 km long system of tunnels to connect all major defense installations. By the time the Americans landed, 13 km had been completed. The work was extremely hard: temperatures ranged from 30 to 50 degrees Celsius, gas masks had to be worn against the sulphurous fumes, and from 8 December the American air force bombed the island daily. Despite the American blockade by submarines and bombers, reinforcements kept trickling in. Eventually, General Kuribayashi had 21,000 to 23,000 men at his disposal.

His defense plan differed radically from all previous plans for defending the island:

- In order not to betray their positions, Japanese artillery would not answer American ship shelling.
- They wouldn't catch the Americans on the beaches.
- 400 to 500 meters inland, the Americans would come under fire from automatic weapons at the airfield and artillery on the volcano Suribachi and from the high ground to the north.
- After inflicting maximum damage, the artillery of the airfield would be withdrawn to the north.
- There would be no major *banzai* counterattack.
- There would be an elastic, sedentary defense. The Japanese troops had supplies for 2.5 months.

American preparation

On October 7, 1944, Admiral Chester W. Nimitz and his staff formulated the objectives for Operation Detachment. The overall goal for the operation was against Japan "to keep the pressure on" and to consolidate American control of the Pacific. With Iwo Jima in American hands, American bombers would be less hampered in their bombing of

Japan, and the island could be used as a base for attacks on Japan. American fighter planes could support American bombers in their flights to Japan, and damaged bombers could make an emergency landing on Iwo Jima.

On October 9, General Holland Smith received the staff study, accompanied by an order from Admiral Chester Nimitz to take control of the island. The order also named the commanders for the operation.

- Admiral Raymond Spruance, commander of the Fifth Fleet, was given command of Operation Commander with Task Force 50.
- Under Spruance fell Vice Admiral Richmond Kelly Turner, commander of amphibious forces in the Pacific, would command Task Force 51.
- Deputy commander of the Joint Expeditionary Force was Rear Admiral Harry W. Hill. General Holland Smith was designated commanding general of the "Expeditionary Troops," Task Force 56.

It was not by chance that these individuals were chosen for this operation. Each of them had earned their spurs in previous similar operations. It was the team that had organized and perfected amphibious techniques from Guadalcanal to Guam and from the Solomon Islands to Tarawa.

The main units of the landing force would be the 3rd, 4th, and 5th Divisions of Marines. The 3rd Division had already distinguished itself at Bougainville in the Solomon Islands and on Guam in the Mariana Islands. The division was still reorganizing in the fall of 1944 after the heavy fighting on Guam and also active in clearing the last Japanese pockets of resistance on the island.

Admiral Spruance assumed command of the forces involved in the central Pacific on 26 January. The 4th and 5th Marine divisions minus the 26th regiment were designated for landing. The 26th Regiment was reserve, while the 3rd Division was to embark from Guam and not land until D+3 (three days after the initial landing).

The landing schedule was simple: the 4th and 5th divisions would land on the eastern beach, the 4th on the right and the 5th on the left.The 3rd division would later land on the same beach and play an offensive or defensive role as needed.The plan envisioned a rapid expansion of the bridgehead. A regiment of the 5th division was designated for the capture of the Suribachi volcano to the south.

Because of the risk of adverse wave conditions on the eastern beaches, an alternative plan for landing on the western beaches was drawn up on 8 January 1945. The likelihood that this plan would be implemented was not high, because the prevailing north to northwest winds gave dangerous waves on the western coast of the island.

For the landing the eastern beach was divided into strips of 450 metres (500 yards) which were named from left to right as green,red 1 and 2, yellow 1 and 2 and blue 1 and 2. The 5th Division Marines would land on green and red 1 and 2, and move straight across the island until it reached the west coast: the island was quite narrow at this point. One regiment was to take the volcano Suribachi.

The 4th Marine Division's mission was to capture the center of the island, while its flank was to target the Motoyama Plateau, the high ground overlooking the landing area. Unless both targets, from which the beaches could be randomly strafed, were quickly taken, casualties among the landing forces could quickly mount.

When the southern part of the island had been secured, the two divisions would advance northward together, and the 3rd Division Marines, initially kept on board as reserve, would go ashore to give the attack additional force.

The detailed landing schedule, from left to right:

- **Green 1:** 28th Regiment, Colonel Harry B. Liversedge:
- **Green 1:** 27th Regiment, Colonel Thomas A. Wornham:
- **Yellow 1 and 2:** 23rd Regiment, Colonel Walter W. Wensinger: Capture Motoyama Airfield
- **blue 1:** 25th Regiment, Colonel John R. Lanigan: assisting in taking airfield 1
- 24th Regiment, Colonel Walter I. Jordan, in reserve
- 26th Regiment, Colonel Chester B. Graham: Support 5th Division

The artillery would not go ashore until ordered by the division commander. The 14th regiment (Colonel Louis G. DeHaven) and 13th regiment (Colonel James D. Wailer) would provide support to the 4th and 5th divisions, respectively.

The operation was timed so that at hour U 68 amphibious landing craft from the first wave of attack would arrive on the beach. These vehicles would advance to the first strip of land beyond the high tide line. These armored vehicles would use their howitzers and machine guns to keep the enemy under cover. In this way the infantry would have covering fire from the next waves of attack as they ran from their landing craft across the beach. The timing for the landing of the tanks would be determined flexibly. A three-day bombardment of the island followed from 16 February.

The American landing

At 02:00 a.m. on February 19, American battleships began shelling as at the start of D-Day.A bombardment by a hundred bombers followed, after which the ship's artillery returned to action. At 08.30 hours the first of 30,000 marines went ashore on Iwo Jima.

The marines were under heavy fire from the volcano Suribachi in the south of the island. The terrain in which they fought was extremely hostile: rough volcanic ash on which it was easy to slip, but in which it was not possible to dig in. Nevertheless, by evening 30,000 marines had gone ashore and the mountain had been cut off from the north of the island. Another 40,000 marines would follow in the course of the battle.

The slopes of the volcano Suribachi had to be fought meter for meter. Gunfire was useless against the well entrenched Japanese infantry. With flamethrowers and grenades, the Japanese bunkers were eliminated piece by piece. It took until February 23 before the top was reached. At 10 a.m. Marines of the 28th regiment planted an American flag on the summit.

This event was repeated a few hours later and one of the most famous photographs of the Second World War was taken. Photographer Joe Rosenthal of the Associated Press won several awards with this photograph, including the Pulitzer Prize in 1945.

When the flag was hoisted, however, not all Japanese defensive positions on the volcano had been taken yet. Heavy fighting continued in the following days. General Kuribayashi forbade a major counterattack when Ichimaru requested his permission.

The landing area had been partially secured with the taking of the volcano. Now more marines and heavy equipment were coming ashore. The invasion was extended to take control of the airfields and the rest of the island. In the following weeks the battle over the entire island remained extremely tough. With traditional courage the Japanese fought to the death. Of the 22,000 defenders only 200 men were captured.

Allied forces suffered 21,000 casualties, including 7,000 killed. A quarter of the Medal of Honor awards given to U.S. Marines during World War II were for operations on Iwo Jima. On 26 March 1945 the island was declared safe.

Admiral Chester W. Nimitz would describe the fighting as follows: *Among the men who fought on Iwo Jima, unusual courage was a common trait.*

Impact

The price for Iwo Jima was high on both sides. However, the price was worth it for the Americans. By the end of the war, 2,400 B-29 bombers with 27,000 crew members had made an emergency landing on the island.

The battle of Okinawa

The Battle of Okinawa (Japanese: 沖縄戦, *Okinawa-sen*), Allied code name Operation Iceberg, took place from April 1 to June 22, 1945 in southern Japan between Japanese and American forces.

The Americans landed on the small Kerama Islands near Okinawa on March 26, 1945 and on Okinawa itself on April 1. The battle was called by the locals *tetsu no ame*, "rain of steel". This battle was the first large-scale introduction of the kamikaze phenomenon to the world. On 23 June the last Japanese surrendered after very hard fighting.

Strategic location of Okinawa

Okinawa is the largest island (about 1200 km²) of the Riukiu Islands, about 600 km southwest of Japan's four main islands. Unlike other islands fought over, such as Iwo Jima, it had a large indigenous population.

The strategic importance of Okinawa during the Second World War was considerable. The Americans had "island-hopped" one island after another south of Japan.

American control of Okinawa would effectively cut off Japanese supplies of materials such as oil, iron ore, and rubber from the south, as well as communications between the Japanese mainland and Japanese bases in the South Pacific. The island could also provide a base for an American attack on Japan's main islands. Okinawa was also home to several airfields and the only two reasonably large ports between Formosa and the Japanese main island of Kyushu.

Okinawa during the Great Asian War

There was little evidence of the struggle in China, which began in 1937, on the island. It had never been an industrial area and it had never produced much food. The only Okinawa contribution lay in the fact that sugar cane was grown on the island, from which alcohol could be produced for torpedoes and engines.

However, when the United States became involved in the war through the attack on Pearl Harbor on December 7, 1941, the island was fortified. It became a cornerstone in the "defensive wall" of Japan. Several airfields were built and the ports were modernized to accommodate large warships and aircraft carriers.

Operation Iceberg

Troop strength

- American forces in the Pacific had already taken several islands, most recently Iwo Jima and the Philippines. Admiral Raymond A. Spruance's American Fifth Fleet had more than forty aircraft carriers, eighteen battleships, two hundred destroyers, and hundreds of ships of all types for support (e.g., corvettes and hospital ships). In all, about 1,300 United States ships surrounded the island. Of those 1,300, 365 were amphibious ships.
- The newly assembled U.S. 10th Army, which entered the battle for Okinawa on April 1, 1945 with 154,000 men, consisted of seven of the most hardened divisions fighting in the Pacific. The 14th Corps under General John Hodge consisted of the 7th and 96th infantry divisions; Major General Roy Stanley Geiger's Third Amphibious Corps consisted of the 1st and 6th Marine divisions; the

27th and 77th infantry divisions and the 2nd Marine Division made up the reserve force.

- As with Iwo Jima, American intelligence underestimated the strength of the enemy on Okinawa. The reason for this was that, when they prepared the attack, the island was still too far away for American reconnaissance planes. The number of Japanese was estimated at 65,000, while it turned out to be more than 100,000. B-29 bombers carried out the first reconnaissance mission over Okinawa and surrounding islands.
- The Japanese Imperial Army under Mitsuru Ushijima had a defense plan ready. Because of the overwhelming American supremacy at sea and in the air it was decided not to fight on the beaches. Almost the entire north of the island was left undefended, with the exception of Mount Yaedake, Kadena airfield and the bases at Yomitan. In the mountainous area of southern Okinawa, however, four defensive circles, known as Shuri circles, were established in which the Japanese dug in. The Shuri circles were easily defensible thanks to the rugged landscape and the large numbers of Japanese artillery of various calibres.

The fleet arrives

On October 10, 1944, approximately two hundred planes on the orders of Admiral Halsey bombed Naha, the largest city and capital of Okinawa. The city was almost completely destroyed. In mid-March 1945 the American fleet assembled to bomb Okinawa. The first kamikazes also appeared.

The landing

Before the army landed, the ships of Task Force 52 led by General Blandy bombed the beaches with 13,000 shells. Furthermore Curtis Lemay's bombers carried out 3000 sorties. The Americans expected to eliminate almost all resistance on the island before the actual landing. The fleet bombardment did not stop before the first American soldiers set foot ashore, meeting almost no resistance. At the end of the first day almost 60,000 American soldiers (two marine divisions and two army divisions) had landed.

At the same time as the first wave of attacks, the Second Marine Division had carried out a diversionary action to the south. On the second day the same action was carried out so that the Japanese could not prevent a bridgehead from being formed at the landing site. The Americans quickly moved across the island and isolated the south from the north, still without encountering noteworthy resistance.

The follow-up to the landing took place in four phases:

- The advance to the eastern coast (1-4 April).
- Exploring and taking the northern part of the island (April 5-18).
- Taking the surrounding islands (April 10 - June 26).
- The actual battle with the entrenched Japanese 32nd Army. This battle began on April 6 and did not end until June 21.

The battles

The battle in southern Okinawa contrasted with the rapid capture of the north of the island.

Only when the 7th and 96th infantry divisions were sent south, because the Americans heard from natives that the Japanese were mainly in the south, did the real battle for Okinawa begin.

Ultimately, the battle of Okinawa became one of the bloodiest and most bitter battles of the entire war.

Although the Americans met with determined resistance on 5 April, the advance was still able to proceed, albeit with difficulty. By 9 April, resistance was so strong that both Roy Stanley Geiger's and John Hodge's divisions came to a complete halt in front of a heavily defended position on the Kakazuberg Ridge. The Americans attacked for days, supported by B-29 Superfortress bombers, but were continually repulsed.

There were many casualties on the Japanese side. On April 12, the day American president Roosevelt died, more than 5,500 Japanese were killed, against 'only' 451

Americans. However, the Americans were still facing the Kakazuberg Ridge.

The first three defensive circles fell relatively easily. The fact that the Japanese launched tactically unwise counterattacks worked to the Americans' advantage.

But at the fourth circle on Kiyamuschiere Island, resistance was very bitter. When all hope was lost, several Japanese, including General Mitsuru Ushijima, committed seppuku or blew themselves up with hand grenades.

Losses

- American losses: Some 34 ships sank, 368 ships were damaged, 763 planes were shot down. In all, more than 12,000 American soldiers were killed during the Battle of Okinawa.
- Japanese losses: Japanese losses were enormous. 107,539 soldiers died, 10,755 were captured or surrendered. 7830 planes and sixteen ships were destroyed.
- Civilian casualties: Residents of Okinawa were forced into the Japanese army and died in the fighting. Many others fled to caves to avoid being caught in shelling and were buried alive in collapses there. Artillery and aerial bombardments also caused many casualties. All estimates are between one third and one tenth of the population.
- A phenomenon that should not be underestimated is the so-called "battlestress". This caused more casualties in this battle than in other battles where this phenomenon was also recorded. The repeated attacks, the continuous shelling and the high percentage of deaths are the cause of this. In total there were more than 26.000 psychiatric victims on the American side. On the Japanese side no figures are available.

Kamikaze

The kamikazes are soldiers who try to inflict as many enemy casualties as possible by committing suicide. Most famous are the kamikaze pilots - which were also the most common - but cases of kamikazemini-diveboats, kamikazespeedboats, and kamikaze assaults (in which enclosed soldiers who saw no chance of victory threw themselves at the enemy in a blind rush) are well known. The kamikazes get special mention since the pinnacle of kamikaze attacks occurred during the Battle of Okinawa.

- On 6 and 7 April a massive kamikaze attack took place for the first time. Hundreds of kamikaze planes, the so-called "kikusui" (floating chrysanthemum, the imperial symbol of Japan), attacked the invasion fleet. By the end of the battle, 1465 kamikaze flights had taken place. Thirty American ships were sunk and 164 were damaged.
- The Japanese had also devised a plan to attack the American fleet with fast motorboats full of explosives. However, this plan was never carried out.

- The pride of the Japanese fleet, the *Yamato*, the largest battleship ever, was also sent on a kamikaze mission. The plan was that it would run itself aground on the beaches of Okinawa and act as an artillery emplacement. However, the US submarine *USS Hackleback* detected the battleship and its escort - consisting of the light cruiser *Yahagi* and eight destroyers - earlier and relayed their location. Vice Admiral Marc Mitscher launched air strikes at 10 a.m. on 7 April. During the next two hours the Japanese flotilla was under constant air attack. The *Yamato* took twelve bombs and seven torpedoes. Eventually it exploded and sank. The *Yahagi* and one of the destroyers shared its fate. Four of the other destroyers were unable to return to Japan. Only 269 of the *Yamato*'s crew of 2747 survived the sea battle. The *Yahagi* lost 446 men and on the destroyers 391 died. The Americans lost ten planes and twelve soldiers. This was the last action of the Japanese fleet during the war.

Consequences

The dogged fighting and, by American standards, extremely high losses over a relatively small island gave the Americans little courage or hope for an invasion by conventional means of Japan's main islands. That was precisely the intention of the Japanese supreme command.

This contributed to President Harry Truman's decision to drop the secretly developed atomic bombs on Hiroshima and Nagasaki. According to popular belief, Emperor Hirohito was thus forced to capitulate. This marked the end of the Second World War, because Germany had already capitulated in May 1945.

End of the war

With the collapse of Nazi Germany in May 1945, the Americans wanted to end the war in Asia as soon as possible. It was agreed with the Soviet Union that it would cancel the non-aggression pact with Japan and declare war after 3 months (i.e. August 8, 1945).

Despite heavy bombing of Japanese cities, Japan refused to surrender. To force Japan to surrender, without enormous losses on their own side by an invasion of Japan, the Americans decided to use a new weapon: the atomic bomb. On August 6, the first atomic bomb, nicknamed *Little Boy*, fell on Hiroshima. A few days later, August 9, the *Fat Man* bomb followed, falling on Nagasaki. One day before the atomic attack on Nagasaki, the Soviet Union had declared war on Japan. On 9 August the Soviet Union launched Operation August Storm: 1.5 million men entered Manchuria (Manchukwo), Inner Mongolia (Mengjiang), South Sakhalin (Karafuto), North Korea and, on 18 August, the Kurils. The surprised Japanese offered little resistance and over a million men, including 180 generals, were taken prisoner of war. Russian paratroopers also managed to arrest the puppet emperor of Manchuria, Pu Yi.

At 11 p.m. on 14 August, Japan informed the Allies by telegram that it accepted the terms of the Potsdam Declaration and those contained in U.S. Secretary of State James F. Byrnes' letter of 11 August.

With that, Japan had surrendered. A day later at noon the news of Japan's surrender was announced by the Emperor over the radio, but the Soviets continued their advance until September 1 and captured the Kurils. On September 2, Japan signed the Act of Surrender on the battleship *Missouri*. This ended World War II.

At the concluded peace, Japan ceded several Japanese territories:

- its mandate over the formerly German Pacific Islands (independent)
- the southern half of Sakhalin Island (to the Soviet Union)
- the Kurils (to the Soviet Union)
- the South Manchurian Railway (China)
- Taiwan (China)

Aftermath

The end of World War II was followed by a shock wave of war-induced changes in East Asia.

In China, shortly after World War II, a civil war broke out between the nationalist government of Chiang Kai-shek and the communists of Mao Tsetung. In 1949 the communists won and the People's Republic of China was founded. The nationalists fled to Formosa, where they continued the Republic of China, now better known as Taiwan.

In the Dutch East Indies the Japanese occupation led to the emergence of an independence movement and on 17 August 1945 the Dutch colony declared itself independent as the Republic of Indonesia, with Sukarno as its first president. Years of guerrilla warfare followed, which the Netherlands responded to with the so-called police actions, until the Netherlands, under American pressure, recognised the independence of Indonesia on 27 December 1949.

Korea was divided after World War II into a northern, communist part, supported by the Soviet Union, and a southern part, supported by the United States. In 1950, North Korea invaded the southern part, South Korea. A United Nations force defended South Korea, upon which the new People's Republic of China intervened on the North Korean side. In 1953 an armistice was concluded between North and South Korea, which has continued until today.

Nationalists also seized their chance in the French colony of Vietnam. Soon after the end of the Second World War a guerrilla war broke out between the French and the nationalists, the beginning of the Vietnam War. In 1949 the French had to recognise Vietnam's independence. However, the conflict with the communist Vietminh of Hồ Chí Minh continued and in 1950 Ho Chi Minh declared North Vietnam independent. In 1957 war broke out between North Vietnam and US-backed South Vietnam, a war in which the Americans became increasingly involved.

www.ingramcontent.com/pod-product-compliance
Lightning Source LLC
LaVergne TN
LVHW020032160726
843469LV00044B/1736

* 9 7 8 9 4 9 3 2 9 8 7 7 4 *